SANDY KOUFAX

The lefty who changed the Game

SHAWN BLAKE

TABLE OF CONTENTS:

INTRODUCTION

Are you an enthusiast for baseball? Has there ever been a pitcher so outstanding that hitters could not make contact with his fastball?

Allow me to present to you Sandy Koufax, the one and only left-handed pitcher that permanently altered baseball history!

Picture this: the stadium is full on a sweltering summer day. The pitcher's mound is the center of attention for everyone.

Abruptly, a towering left-handed pitcher approaches and fixes his gaze on the hitter. He fires a lightning fastball that appears to be shooting out of a cannon in a single motion! It was Koufax, Sandy.

However, did you know that Sandy wasn't always a baseball superstar from the beginning?

Nope! Before, he was a typical young boy dreaming of making it to the major leagues while playing catch in his neighborhood.

And what do you know? He had no idea if he would be competent at it! His path to becoming one of the all-time great pitchers was paved with heart, hard work, ups and downs, and a lot of perseverance.

So prepare yourself and grab your glove! We're delving into Sandy Koufax's fascinating biography in this book.

You're about to meet the lefty who rose to fame, from his humble beginnings in Brooklyn to the electrifying environment of a sold-out stadium. Raise the bat!

CHAPTER 1: The Early Days

Not everyone knew Sandy Koufax as the well-known pitcher with an incredible arm. Initially, he was just an ordinary child growing up in Brooklyn, New York. Sandy, who was born in 1935, dreamed of becoming a professional athlete and spent his early years playing stickball with his buddies and dashing through the congested streets.

But baseball was not his first love, what was it, and can you guess? Basketball! You did read correctly! Before Sandy ever threw a curveball, he was a star basketball player.

He was an expert at passing, dribbling, and shooting baskets. His friends thought he was going to be the next big thing in basketball.

However, life has a humorous way of throwing us curveballs, and Sandy's path was about to take an unexpected detour.

While Sandy was playing with his friends one lovely afternoon, someone said, "Hey, Sandy, why don't you try pitching?" He laughed it off at first.

After all, he was an avid hoops fan. However, when he did finally pick up that baseball and give it a try, the ball shot into the air at an incredible pace! His friends were in disbelief.

They said, "Whoa, did you see that?" Sandy had found his latent gift! Sandy didn't spend much time on the baseball field before he started throwing fastballs to anyone who was daring enough to catch them.

However, it wasn't simple. Occasionally, he would toss the ball in such a way that it would go over the catcher's head—too high, too low, or wildly! But Sandy persisted in her practice instead of giving up.

He practiced his throws every day, pushing himself to get better. He quickly gained notoriety in his community as the "kid with the golden arm."

Nobody realized that this was only the start of a journey that would permanently alter baseball.

CHAPTER 2: A Young Pitcher's Dream

Sandy Koufax's passion for baseball grew along with him. He possessed strength and speed, but most of all, he had the dream.

Sandy would practice his pitches on the neighborhood ball fields in Brooklyn every evening after school.

Occasionally, he would remain until the sun set behind the skyline of the city, not leaving until he perfected his fastball.

People had been talking about Sandy, the "kid pitcher," who could hurl the ball faster than anyone they had ever seen, by the time she got to high school.

At his games, scouts from nearby baseball organizations started showing up, whispering to one another with excitement each time he threw another scorching fastball.

Sandy was still just a youngster figuring out what he wanted to do with his life, but his reputation was growing.

Sandy was once contacted by his coach, who told him, "Koufax, you have a talent that only comes once in a lifetime." You ought to consider playing professionally, perhaps even in the major leagues someday.

The thought caused Sandy's heart to speed. The major leagues? Taking a pro baseball team to bat?

Though it seemed like a dream come true, he was a little anxious. Was he going to make it?

However, Sandy never backs down from a challenge. He decided to give baseball his all as a result. Every pitch, drill, and match.

He was curious to find out how far he could go with his arm. And what a crazy journey it was going to be!

He chose to test out for the local semi-pro teams after high school, and you know what happened? He was quite popular!

Watching him pitch, spectators flocked to the bleachers, holding their breath as he geared up to throw.

Every time the ball raced through the air and struck the catcher's glove with a loud *pop!*, you could hear the gasps of astonishment. It resembled magic.

But Sandy had moved past simple play. His sights were set on the opportunity to play in the major leagues.

He had a dream of feeling the thrill of a full stadium as he took the mound in front of thousands of screaming spectators.

One day, following an especially exciting game, a Brooklyn Dodgers scout came up to him.

Sandy received a pat on the back from the scout who stated, "Kid, you've got something special." Would you like to become a member of the Brooklyn Dodgers? Sandy felt her heart almost skip a beat.

The Dodgers, perhaps? The squad he'd watched since childhood? It was practically too amazing to be true! Breathing deeply, he met the scout's gaze and said, "Let's do it."

After that, Sandy Koufax set out to pursue his greatest ambition to date: turning pro in baseball.

He had no idea that the road ahead would be full of both successes and setbacks and that he would need to put in more effort than ever to develop into the pitcher who would alter the course of baseball forever.

CHAPTER 3: Chasing the Big League

For Sandy Koufax, signing with the Brooklyn Dodgers was a dream come true, but he found that life in the major leagues wasn't as simple as he had thought.

Sandy discovered he wasn't the best player on the field as soon as he got to the Dodgers' training camp.

He could see towering pitchers, quick outfielders, and hard-hitting batters everywhere he looked.

It felt as though one had entered a whole new realm of skill. Sandy had to endure exhausting practice sessions with the coaches.

He worked on his pitching every day, attempting to figure out the best technique to outwit batters, the ideal grip for the ball, and the appropriate arm angle.

The thing is, though: Sandy was crazy, his throws could occasionally fly out of control because they were so rapid!

He could toss a pitch with lightning speed one minute, then the next, it would fly over the catcher's head or bounce off the ground. Coaches would yell, "Control, Sandy, control!" "Speed is great, but you've got to aim that rocket arm of yours!"

Sandy was aware of their accuracy. Being able to control your fastball was far more important than just possessing a strong one.

He was much more determined to practice as a result. After every training session, he stayed late to refine his pitches.

He persisted even though his legs felt like jello and his arm hurt. He was pursuing the greatest dream of his life, after all.

Sandy had the opportunity to play in a few games during his first season with the Dodgers, but things didn't go exactly as expected.

His nervousness seemed to get the better of him with every pitch. With the enormous crowd and intense pressure, Sandy found it difficult to maintain his concentration.

His wayward pitches made things simple for the batters, and before he knew it, the other team was racking up hits all over the place.

Nor were the newspapers kind. It was difficult to ignore headlines like "Dodgers' Rookie Pitcher Needs Work" and "Koufax Struggles on the Mound." Sandy was irritated.

Here he was, a young man who had grown up dreaming of being a major league player, but now he had to face his uncertainties. Is he truly going to be a successful professional pitcher? Sandy, though, was not about to give up.

He was aware that hardships were a part of being a great player. He would tell himself in the changing room, "Even legends start somewhere."

He thus kept on exercising, paying attention to his coaches, and growing from every error. They helped him with his technique, showing him how to manage his scorching fastball and how to handle the ball for other pitches.

Then something started to shift. He gained a little more knowledge with every game. His confidence gradually returned, and his pitches became more accurate.

Sandy started to realize that being a great pitcher required more than just the fastest throw; it also required understanding the game, outwitting the hitter, and maintaining composure under duress.

The throng also observed it. At one game, the fans got up to applaud the rookie pitcher who was starting to get into a groove after he struck out three straight batters.

Sandy experienced the exhilaration of the roaring crowd for the first time. It was just a tiny taste of the goal he had been pursuing with great effort.

However, this was just the start. Sandy realized he was still a long way from being the pitcher he had always imagined himself to be.

He would need to never give up, never stop learning, and most of all, never stop having faith in himself. He was prepared to face every challenge on the difficult path to greatness.

He had no idea that those early setbacks would serve as the cornerstone of a career that would soon become baseball history!

CHAPTER 4: Becoming a Dodger

Sandy Koufax was gradually developing into a legitimate contender on the Dodgers team, going from a rookie with a crazy arm to a contender with every game.

Although the journey wasn't simple, it was undoubtedly thrilling! Now that he was playing with some of the biggest names in baseball, Sandy had a surge of excitement each time he put on that blue Dodger uniform.

He was now a Dodger officially—this was it! Nevertheless, Sandy's path had its ups and downs even as a team member.

He was still getting used to finding his groove in those early years. On certain days, he would take the mound and pitch like a pro, effortlessly striking out batters.

His name would be chanted by the raucous assembly, "Kou-fax! Kou-fax!" And he thought he could take on the world on those days.

Then there were the days that weren't so good.
Occasionally, he would unleash his furious
pitches once again, missing the strike zone by a
considerable distance, and the hitters would
capitalize by smacking his fastballs out of the
park.

The coaches' booming voices could be heard
throughout the stadium as they yelled, "Control,
Sandy!" from the dugout.

He began to gain notoriety as an erratic pitcher who might be excellent at times or not.

When Sandy took the mound, spectators were never quite sure what to expect from the man known by reporters as "the mystery arm." Would they be able to witness the pitcher with lightning-fast strikes? Or the one who found it difficult to wield authority? Sandy, though, persisted in moving forward.

Even though he hadn't completely sorted everything out yet, he felt he had the potential to be something amazing.

He collaborated extensively with the Dodgers' instructors, who taught him new pitching motions and how to read batters.

They showed him that pitching success required more than just throwing as hard as you could; it also required planning and accuracy.

Sandy was pulled aside by a coach one day. "You possess an innate talent," he stated, putting his hand on Sandy's shoulder.

It's time to make that gift work for you, though, immediately. Let us consider control. Let's give each pitch some weight.

For Sandy, that was the pivotal moment. He understood that his arm was a tool he had to learn how to use, not merely something he could use quickly.

Sandy returned to her job. He worked on his curveball, a deceptive pitch that could mislead even the most skilled hitters, every day.

The curveball required skill in addition to power. It needed the right timing and a precise grip.

Sandy didn't give up even if his curveballs first faltered and missed their mark. He practiced pitch after pitch until he started to acquire the feel of it.

His curveball soon turned into a weapon. One game, he stepped onto the mound and sent the ball whirling toward home plate with a flick of his wrist.

Expecting a fastball, the batter swung, but the ball unexpectedly bent and dove straight past his bat and into the catcher's glove.

The umpire yelled, "Strike three!" as the audience went wild with applause. Sandy had succeeded in enhancing his repertoire with a fresh, nearly enchanted pitch.

Sandy started to get attention for her performances that season. With his improved control, he struck out batters, leading the crowds to think he was more than simply "the mystery arm."

As a pitcher for the Dodgers, he was growing into a real force. The newspapers also took a different stance. They were now penning tales about "the rising star, Sandy Koufax."

Still, Sandy refused to let the accolades get to his head. He was aware that every game was an opportunity for growth and validation.

He told himself, "One step at a time," before each game. "Just keep pushing, keep learning." And he carried out that exact action.

He became more adept at handling pressure as he pitched more. The intensity of the fans, the lighting in the stadium, and the batters' looks motivated him to improve.

Sandy Koufax was becoming a Dodger, but he was also gradually becoming a pitcher who would have a lasting impact on the sport.

But he had no idea how high he was about to soar as his trip was just getting started. There were still obstacles to overcome, conflicts to engage in, and records to smash.

Sandy Koufax was about to go on an amazing journey, and the baseball community was about to experience an exhilarating encounter!

CHAPTER 5: Struggles on the Mound

Sandy Koufax knew he had a steep uphill struggle ahead of him as he pursued his career with the Dodgers.

He struggled on the mound even with his moments of brilliance. One day, his fastball and curveball would dazzle fans as he pitched an almost flawless game.

The next time, he would struggle to maintain control and toss wild pitches that were well outside the strike zone.

It was exhilarating at high points and terrifying at low points, similar to being on a roller coaster.

Because they never quite knew which Sandy would appear on any given day, the spectators in the stands were frequently on the edge of their seats.

They understood he wasn't quite the unstoppable force they thought he could be, even if they still loved him.

What about the newspapers? Yes, they were ready to call attention to all of his errors. "Koufax Can't Find His Groove" and "Dodgers' Star Still Searching for Control" were the headlines.

Although it was difficult to read, Sandy did not give up. He only needed to discover it within himself since he knew he was capable of greatness.

One word that described Sandy's troubles frequently was control. Although he had a faster throw than nearly everyone else in the league, a fastball would be useless if it didn't go where he intended it to.

He put in a lot of effort to rediscover his rhythm in every game, but the pressure was great.

He could feel the weight of the entire stadium following his every move as he stood on the pitcher's mound.

At moments, it was all so overwhelming—the umpire's calls, the crowd's cheers, and the crack of the bat.

"Remain concentrated," he would remind himself. "One pitch at a time, please." Still, it was easier said than done. Several times, after giving up home runs or walking too many batters, he found himself heading back to the dugout with his head hanging low.

And his frustration increased with each hard game. He questioned, "Why can't I get it right?" "What have I overlooked?" His coaches made an effort to assist.

He received instruction on improving his pitching mechanics, including stance, grip, and windup adjustments. "Sandy, calm down," they said. "Avoid attempting to dominate each pitch.

Have faith in your gut feelings. Even with his expertise and attentive listening, there were days when nothing seemed to fit.

He was not without talent; in fact, he possessed an abundance of it. What he was missing was consistency.

Sandy sat by himself in the locker room with his head in his hands one day during an especially difficult outing in which he walked four batters in a row.

He started to question whether he would ever be the pitcher he had always imagined himself to be for the first time. Perhaps he was destined to be just another talented player who was never able to reach the big time.

But then there was a stir inside him. Standing on the mound in Major League Baseball, he considered his entire journey thus far, from the young boy playing stickball in the streets of Brooklyn to the present.

He came to see that there was never a direct path to greatness. There were many curves, twists, and bumps in the road.

He proclaimed out loud, "I'm not giving up," and got to his feet with newfound vigor. "I'm going to solve this problem." After that, he prepared to work even harder and returned to the practice field.

Sandy dissected each of his pitches, concentrating on the fundamentals. He practiced all the little things that could help him regain control, such as his release point, grip, and windup.

He observed how other pitchers handled difficult circumstances and maintained their composure while on the mound for hours on end.

He developed his strategic thinking skills by learning to read batters and vary his pitches to keep them off balance.

The pieces started to fit together gradually. He faced an especially difficult batter in one game.

Three balls and two strikes made up the 3-2 count. Everything would depend on the next pitch. Sandy inhaled deeply, turned, and threw a flawless curveball.

After swinging, the batter missed! Triple strike! As the crowd erupted, Sandy briefly experienced the exhilaration of accomplishment.

It took time for the transition to occur. He continued to have terrible games and days when he was unable to get into a rhythm.

But the talented pitcher within him was beginning to show itself, little by little. He gained the ability to move past his errors and persevere in the face of setbacks.

Sandy had a difficult day on the mound, no question about it. However, they were also molding him, instilling in him the values of resiliency, persistence, and never losing hope in his abilities.

He was being prepared for something bigger than he could have ever imagined by this fight, which he was unaware of at the time.

Sandy Koufax's actual potential was yet unknown to the world, but he would overcome these obstacles and go on to become a genuine baseball icon.

CHAPTER 6: Finding His Rhythm

Sandy Koufax had a long and difficult road to becoming a pitcher's mound virtuoso, but he was finally starting to settle into a groove.

After years of effort and anguish, things began to make sense. His self-doubt, coaching advice, and endless hours on the practice field were all working together to make him a more composed and astute pitcher.

His perspective on pitching was one significant adjustment. Before, Sandy would attempt to use his extraordinary speed to overwhelm every batter.

He believed that success would come easily if he just threw hard enough. But now, he was discovering that becoming a great pitcher required more than just speed—it also required smartness.

He began to view pitching as a chess game in which every throw required meticulous consideration and preparation.

Sandy started experimenting with various pitch ranges. Although he possessed his renowned fastball, he required more tools in his repertoire to keep hitters off balance.

He put in endless hours honing his curveball until it was a thing of beauty, a pitch so unpredictable that hitters would swing at the air, confused by the ball's abrupt drop.

To keep batters guessing, he also worked on changing the tempo of his pitches. They would be ready for a fastball at one moment and be tricked by a sluggish, looping curveball the next.

It resembled magic. However, control was equally as important as the pitches. Sandy developed the ability to throw strikes with accuracy, focusing on the corners of the strike zone where it would be most difficult for batters to make firm contact.

Now he could direct the ball to travel in whatever direction he pleased—high, low, inside, or outside. On the mound, the untamed, erratic pitcher he once was, was evolving into a skilled artisan.

Next came the 1961 season, which was Sandy's career's turning point. He gave a performance that stunned everyone during a game against the Cincinnati Reds.

He tied the National League record for the most strikeouts in a single game with 18, having struck out 18 batters. There was electricity in the stadium.

Every strikeout sent the fans to their feet, and the reporters could not stop taking notes. Something clicked in Sandy at that same instant.

He was now controlling the game, not merely throwing the ball. Finding his rhythm gave him a rush he had never experienced before.

The birth of the pitcher he was destined to be seemed to be the culmination of years of struggle.

Within the league, word of his incredible feats started to circulate. When Sandy was on the mound, Batters walked fearfully up to the plate.

They were aware that they would be facing off against his ferocious fastballs and cunning curveballs. and Sandy? He was having the time of his life.

He'd settled into a groove that gave him the assurance and accuracy he needed to pitch. His teammates also observed the shift. "Here comes Koufax," they would nudge one another in the dugout.

Keep an eye on this. The Dodgers' pitching ace seemed to have something unique, and there was a fresh buzz in the locker room.

Anything was possible, they thought, with Sandy on the mound. As the season progressed, Sandy remained in charge.

He knocked out batter after batter in game after game, helping the Dodgers win series after series. And his reputation got stronger with each pitch and each strikeout.

He became known as "The Left Arm of God," a
moniker that perfectly encapsulated his
legendary presence on the field.

However, Sandy maintained he modesty. He was
aware that his improved rhythm wasn't the
product of magic, but rather many hours of
dedication, effort, and patience.

At last, he had discovered how to use his gift, fusing instinctive strength with discipline and planning.

And it was yielding results beyond his wildest expectations. Sandy Koufax was more than just a fast-ball throwing pitcher by the end of the season; he was a formidable force.

He was on the fast track to greatness now that he had discovered his rhythm. But he knew in his heart that this was only the beginning.

There were still obstacles to overcome, records to shatter, and history to be written. For the first time, though, he felt that he was prepared to face any challenge that came his way.

Sandy Koufax's entire genius was yet unknown to the baseball world, but one thing was for sure: the lefty had found his groove and was turning games around pitch by pitch.

Sandy Koufax had a long and difficult road to becoming a pitcher's mound virtuoso, but he was finally starting to settle into a groove.

After years of effort and anguish, things began to make sense. His self-doubt, coaching advice, and endless hours on the practice field were all working together to make him a more composed and astute pitcher.

His perspective on pitching was one significant adjustment. Before, Sandy would attempt to use his extraordinary speed to overwhelm every batter.

He believed that success would come easily if he just threw hard enough. But now he was discovering that becoming a great pitcher required more than just speed—it also required smartness.

He began to view pitching as a chess game in which every throw required meticulous consideration and preparation.

Sandy started experimenting with various pitch ranges. Although he possessed his renowned fastball, he required more tools in his repertoire to keep hitters off balance.

He put in endless hours honing his curveball until it was a thing of beauty, a pitch so unpredictable that hitters would swing at the air, confused by the ball's abrupt drop.

To keep batters guessing, he also worked on changing the tempo of his pitches. They would be ready for a fastball at one moment and be tricked by a sluggish, looping curveball the next.

It resembled magic. However, control was equally as important as the pitches. Sandy developed the ability to throw strikes with accuracy, focusing on the corners of the strike zone where it would be most difficult for batters to make firm contact.

Now he could direct the ball to travel in whatever direction he pleased—high, low, inside, or outside.

On the mound, the untamed, erratic pitcher he once was was evolving into a skilled artisan.

Next came the 1961 season, which was Sandy's career's turning point. He gave a performance that stunned everyone during a game against the Cincinnati Reds.

He tied the National League record for the most strikeouts in a single game with 18, having struck out 18 batters.

There was electricity in the stadium. Every strikeout sent the fans to their feet, and the reporters could not stop taking notes. Something clicked in Sandy at that same instant.

He was now controlling the game, not merely throwing the ball. Finding his rhythm gave him a rush he had never experienced before.

The birth of the pitcher he was destined to be seemed to be the culmination of years of struggle.

Within the league, word of his incredible feats started to circulate. When Sandy was on the mound, Batters walked fearfully up to the plate.

They were aware that they would be facing off against his ferocious fastballs and cunning curveballs. And Sandy? He was having the time of his life.

He'd settled into a groove that gave him the assurance and accuracy he needed to pitch. His teammates also observed the shift. "Here comes Koufax," they would nudge one another in the dugout.

Keep an eye on this. The Dodgers' pitching ace seemed to have something unique, and there was a fresh buzz in the locker room. Anything was possible, they thought, with Sandy on the mound.

As the season progressed, Sandy remained in charge. He knocked out batter after batter in game after game, helping the Dodgers win series after series.

And his reputation got stronger with each pitch and each strikeout. He became known as "The Left Arm of God," a moniker that perfectly encapsulated his legendary presence on the field.

However, Sandy maintained her modesty. He was aware that his improved rhythm wasn't the product of magic, but rather many hours of dedication, effort, and patience.

At last, he had discovered how to use his gift, fusing instinctive strength with discipline and planning.

And it was yielding results beyond his wildest expectations. Sandy Koufax was more than just a fast-ball throwing pitcher by the end of the season; he was a formidable force.

He was on the fast track to greatness now that he had discovered his rhythm. But he knew in his heart that this was only the beginning.

There were still obstacles to overcome, records to shatter, and history to be written. For the first time, though, he felt that he was prepared to face any challenge that came his way.

Sandy Koufax's entire genius was yet unknown to the baseball world, but one thing was for sure: the lefty had found his groove and was turning games around pitch by pitch.

CHAPTER 7: The Perfect Lefty

Now that Sandy Koufax had established his rhythm, he was utilizing it to a whole new degree.

With his lightning-fast fastball and devastating curveball under control, Sandy was quickly making a name for himself as the pitcher that opposing teams feared most.

He was not only pitching well by 1963 but perfectly. Sandy Koufax was about to introduce the baseball world to a left-handed pitcher unlike any other.

Sandy took the mound for a game against the San Francisco Giants on a warm summer's evening.

The stadium was buzzing with excitement, with the stands crammed to capacity. All eyes were fixed on the field, anticipating the young pitcher's next move.

Sandy was composed, determined, and prepared to perform for a lifetime. It was evident from the start of the game that something exceptional was taking place.

Sandy was in perfect control of every pitch. His curveballs danced past the hitters, leaving them swinging at nothing but air, while his fastballs shot through the air like rockets.

He easily took out the Giants lineup with one, two, or three outs. The supporters began to feel as though they were watching history unfold as the game went on.

Someone in the audience murmured, "He's throwing a masterpiece." They were correct, too. Sandy was ablaze.

He had struck out almost every batter he faced by the sixth inning, and not a single one had managed to get a hit.

Tension was in the Giants dugout. Knowing they were up against the best in the game, batters gripped their bats nervously as they peered out at Sandy.

But Sandy remained composed and concentrated. Even though he was aware of the stakes, he remained composed.

He ignored the crowd's clamor and the anxiety in the air, approaching each pitch as if it were his first.

He appeared to hone his skill with each throw, adding an extra measure of force and accuracy that astounded everyone.

The ninth inning then started. Holding his breath, the stadium watched Sandy stand atop the mound.

He would record a no-hitter, something most pitchers can only hope to accomplish if he could get three more outs.

This was not your average no-hitter, though; it was a perfect game. Not a single walk, hit, or mistake. Simply put, amazing pitching talent. Stepping up to the plate was the first batter.

With a blistering fastball in his hand, Sandy wound up and—strike one! The assembly let forth a yell.

He made the same move again, curving a curveball past the bat with a dip that made it strike two!.

Sandy gave the hitter one more pitch and struck him out, seeing to it that he was powerless.

Two down, one to go. The following batter was also completely overwhelmed.

Sandy threw a combination of curveballs and fastballs that left him swinging at nothing.

Two free passes. You could almost feel the tension in the air at this point.

The audience seemed tense, with some clenching their fists and holding their breath. The final batter finally stepped up to the plate. Sandy gave him a stern look, his eyes calm and concentrated.

He turned to pitch and unleashed his trademark fastball. After swinging, the batter missed! One down! Taking a deep breath, Sandy wound herself up again and unleashed a nasty curveball that seemed to defy physics with its steep curve.

The hitter struck out once more! Two strikes! This was it, the real deal. Sandy nodded, took one look at the catcher, and got ready for the last pitch. He turned, let go, and launched a fastball down the center.

The batsman gave it his best swing but to no avail. Triple strike! Cheers broke out in the stadium! It was a perfect game pitched by Sandy Koufax! His teammates hurried over to the mound, around him with cheers and bouncing.

Sandy smiled as she absorbed the amazing moment. It was him. Baseball legend, the

Brooklyn boy who once had trouble regaining control.

The following day, headlines like "Koufax the Perfect" and "Sandy Makes History!" flooded the press. Sandy, nevertheless, chose not to let it get to him.

He was prepared for whatever came next as he understood that every game presented a fresh challenge.

Although it was a significant accomplishment, pitching a perfect game was only the first step in his path.

He persisted in challenging himself and aimed for perfection each time he ascended the mound.

Now Sandy Koufax was the ideal left-hander, the guy that hitters dreaded facing.

Even while the baseball community praised him for his accomplishments, Sandy never stopped improving.

He had no idea that he was about to experience even more unforgettable experiences and that his career as one of the greatest pitchers in history was only beginning.

Now at the peak of his game, the lefty who had found it difficult to settle into a groove demonstrated to everyone that anyone could revolutionize the game with a little perseverance,

hard work, and magic in their arm.

CHAPTER 8: Record-Breaking Seasons

Despite having already thrown a perfect game, Sandy Koufax showed no signs of stopping.

His talent, perseverance, and willpower never ceased to astound the baseball community as the seasons went by. Fans expected greatness from Sandy every time he took the mound, and he delivered.

He was developing into an unstoppable force in the league, not merely a fantastic pitcher. Sandy was at the height of his powers in 1963.

His arm was now a powerful, accurate weapon. Every hitter understood that taking on Koufax required rising to an unprecedented level of difficulty.

Sandy had a fantastic season that year. He led the Dodgers to victory after victory with his fastball soaring through the air and his curveball twisting batters into knots.

Then came his momentous encounter with the San Francisco Giants. Sandy struck out 18 batters in just one game, setting a new record for the National League!

Pitch after pitch zipped past batters, who could only shake their heads in shock, leaving the fans in wonder.

Fans cheered loudly as they jumped to their feet upon the final out being called. Sandy had once again left his mark on history. But Sandy wasn't satisfied with just breaking records for strikeouts.

No, his goal was far more ambitious: championship victories. He also assisted in leading the Dodgers to the World Series in that particular year.

He was an amazing sight to witness in the final games. Pitches appeared to possess an independent nature, swiftly slipping past hitters before they could even register a hit.

He set a new record for the most strikeouts in a single World Series game in Game 1 of the Series by striking out 15 batters.

The Dodgers went on to win the pennant, and Sandy received the well-earned title of World Series MVP.

As if that season wasn't enough, Sandy's dominance persisted over the next few years.

He pitched his fourth no-hitter in 1965! But this was perfect; it wasn't just any no-hitter. The opposition club was taken aback when Sandy retired every batter he faced for the second time in his career.

His teammates rushed to congratulate him as he walked off the pitch, causing the stadium to erupt in enthusiasm.

Newspapers praised him as "The Master of the Mound," and sportswriters nationwide were at a loss for words to express how brilliant he was.

Next came the season of 1965, a season that would become legendary. With an astounding 382 strikeouts towards the end of the season,

Sandy set a new Major League Baseball record that would last for years.

It was the most strikeouts a pitcher had ever given up in a season. It appeared as though Sandy was revising the pitching regulations.

He frightened batters worldwide and dazzled fans alike by making the seemingly impossible seem easy.

But Sandy's seasons were legendary for more reasons than just his stats—it was his perseverance and unwavering passion for the game.

He wouldn't slow down, not even when his arm started to hurt and his body started to ache from pitching nonstop.

Driven by his love for the game and his desire to give his squad every opportunity to succeed, he persevered through the agony.

The awards kept coming in. Sandy earned the Cy Young Award three years in a row, which is given to the finest pitcher in baseball.

His status as the dominant pitcher of his era was cemented with each victory. Players and coaches praised him with amazement.

They would say, "He's not just a pitcher; he's a phenomenon." All the accolades and achievements didn't make Sandy any less modest.

It was always about the game, about the team, and about the thrill of throwing for him.

When asked how he was able to be so amazing on the mound, he would smile and respond, "I just go out there and throw."

All were aware, though, that it went beyond simple throwing. His unique combination of skill, diligence, and willpower made him stand out.

Sandy rose to legendary status in the baseball community as he broke records and created history.

Children all around the nation aspired to pitch like Koufax, imitating his windup in their backyards and on neighborhood ball fields.

"Hello, I'm Sandy!" they would exclaim, preparing to deliver their finest fastball.

Furthermore, Sandy's effects extended beyond the field. He turned into an inspiration for commitment, tenacity, and sportsmanship.

He demonstrated to the world that with enough love and work, even the most difficult obstacles could be conquered.

His professional life served as an example of what was possible when one gave their all. Sandy Koufax's seasons of record-breaking success were more than just about winning or statistics.

They told the story of how a young, untamed boy from Brooklyn became a pitcher who altered the course of baseball.

His legacy was created with every pitch, strikeout, and win; it would continue to motivate players and fans for many years to come, even after he threw his last fastball.

But the journey wasn't finished, even though his records were impressive. On and off the pitch, Sandy Koufax still had more to offer, more history to make, and more teachings to impart. His greatness's narrative was far from over.

CHAPTER 9: A True Team Player

Sandy Koufax was a baseball legend on the mound by this point, a superstar, and the best pitcher in the league.

But more than just his skill, what set him apart was the way he approached the game and handled himself.

Being a baseball player meant more to Sandy than just setting records or winning championships; it meant being a good teammate, encouraging his teammates, and giving it his all every time he took the field.

Sandy was regarded as the quiet leader in the Dodgers locker room. He made no demands for preferential treatment or to brag about his accomplishments.

Rather, he motivated his teammates with his dedication to the game and his strong work ethic.

He gave it his all each time he took the mound,

serving the team as well as himself. His

priorities were on doing everything in his power

to help the Dodgers win, not on receiving

personal recognition.

The World Series in 1965 served as the ideal

illustration of Sandy's commitment to his squad.

The Dodgers were playing the formidable Twins

in Minnesota, and the series was sure to be close.

The Dodgers were under pressure to win Game 7 because they needed one more victory to secure the championship. Everyone's gaze was fixed on Sandy.

Sandy was having pain in his arm, and that was the only issue. His body had suffered from years of pitching, and the ache in his left elbow was getting close to excruciating.

But Sandy didn't give up when his team most needed him. He snatched the ball and marched out to the mound with guts and determination, prepared to give it everything he had left.

One of the most courageous pitching outings in the history of the World Series ensued. Sandy pitched through the pain for nine exhausting innings, locating fastballs and curveballs with perfect precision.

The Twins were unable to score because he struck out hitter after batter. As Sandy controlled the game and wouldn't let his team down, the stadium was on the tip of its seat.

The Dodgers had won the World Series, and they hurried to the mound to congratulate their winner after the last out was made.

On one of the biggest stages in sports, Sandy had led his side to victory with a shutout.

Cheers broke out from the crowd as they chanted his name, "Koufax! Koufax!" Despite the festivities, Sandy maintained her modesty.

The success of the squad was more important than his fame. What mattered most was that he had given it his all for them.

Not only did his teammates respect him for his skill, but also for his moral qualities. They would add, "Sandy's the kind of player who makes everyone around him better." "He exemplifies for us what it means to play the game for enjoyment."

Sandy was always happy to help, even off the field. He would give younger pitchers guidance, share insights, and motivate them to keep up their hard work.

Sandy was more than just a fan of his club during games. He chose in 1965 to demonstrate to the world how much he respected his colleagues and his convictions.

Sandy declined to pitch to respect his faith when the World Series' first game fell on Yom Kippur, a major Jewish holiday.

Sandy made a decision that generated media attention, but she stuck with it, demonstrating that certain things in life were more significant than baseball.

The fans and teammates respected him much more for his decision. They witnessed Sandy

Koufax's transformation from a fantastic athlete to a man of character who upheld his moral principles at all costs.

His deeds spoke louder than his feats of feats, demonstrating that a genuine team player put others before himself and adhered to moral standards.

Sandy was the epitome of what it meant to be a good team member. By persevering through discomfort, supporting his teammates, and maintaining his modesty in the face of achievement, he demonstrated that baseball was more than simply a game—it was a means of fostering community.

From his colleagues to the spectators, everyone in his vicinity was inspired by his commitment and devotion.

Sandy carried the attitude of cooperation and friendship with him as he pursued his career.

He was aware that no pitcher, regardless of ability, could secure victory on their own. It needs a team to work together and encourage one another during the highs and lows.

It is what he found so remarkable about being a Dodger, and it is what made the game wonderful.

In addition to his amazing records and accomplishments, Sandy Koufax's legacy was also shaped by the way he played the game—with passion, humility, and devotion to his team.

He changed the game of baseball with his arm as well as his soul, demonstrating what it meant to be a true team player in every game, every inning, and every pitch.

Although Sandy's journey was far from complete, one thing was certain: his brilliance was determined not only by his skill but also by the kind of person and teammate he was. And

for that, he became a multi-dimensional legend.

CHAPTER 10: Facing Challenges

It was the height of Sandy Koufax's career. He had become a baseball legend, broken records, and won titles.

But there are obstacles for even legends. Sandy faced trials that tested his will and passion for the game, including excruciating physical discomfort and tough choices.

It appeared as though nothing could stop Sandy Koufax from the outside. He was viewed by supporters as the unstoppable lefty with unlimited strikeout potential.

Few people understood, though, that Sandy faced more than simply the other team every time he took the mound.

The biggest struggle he had was with his physique. His left arm had suffered from years of pitching at maximum velocity, and by the mid-1960s, the discomfort in his elbow was excruciating.

Sandy used to have arm edema and elbow burns from playing video games. On some days, he could hardly hold a baseball because of how much it hurt.

He would put cold packs on his arm in between innings in the hopes that they would dull the discomfort long enough for the game to go on.

But Sandy never complained, even though it was uncomfortable. Dedicated to providing his squad with his best pitch, he attended every game.

His colleagues gazed in amazement. Shaking their heads, they would add, "I don't know how he does it." "We know he's in pain, but he's pitching like everything is fine."

Sandy concealed her agony from view on the mound. He pitched with everything he had, putting his discomfort aside and concentrating on every hitter and pitch.

However, the suffering worsened as the seasons passed. Doctors determined that he had arthritis, which was causing inflammation in his elbow.

They cautioned him that pitching might cause long-term harm to his arm. For Sandy, this was a devastating blow.

He loved baseball, it was his life, and the idea of having to give it up was unthinkable. Sandy's arm hurt so much after games during the 1966 season that he could hardly raise it.

He nevertheless had one of his best seasons to date. With a 27-9 record in the end, he helped the Dodgers win another National League pennant.

The crowd was in awe as he pitched entire games and knocked out batters, seemingly unaffected by the physical toll it was having on him.

Although it was dubbed "Koufax's miracle season," the cost he was bearing in private was unknown to them.

Sandy was aware that he was at a turning point despite his extraordinary success that year.

The physicians recommended that he think about giving up baseball to protect his long-term health.

It hurt to think of giving up the game he loved. He had dreamed, worked, and become one of the best pitchers of all time on the baseball field, where he had lived his entire life.

Could he truly leave at this point? Sandy struggled to make up her mind. He didn't want to disappoint his supporters or his teammates.

He desired to continue winning games for his squad and throwing. However, he was also aware that if he kept pitching through the excruciating pain, he would never be able to use his arm again.

It was among the hardest decisions he had ever had to make. Sandy ultimately made a choice that demonstrated the depth of his character.

It wasn't that he couldn't dominate on the mound; rather, he decided to quit at the height of his career because he needed to consider life after baseball.

Sandy Koufax, who was only thirty years old, announced his retirement in November 1966.

Around baseball, the news was shocking. How could the game's best pitcher retire so quickly? Sandy merely responded, "I've got a lot of life to live, and I want to be able to enjoy it," when asked about his choice. In that moment of extraordinary power, Sandy demonstrated that being a champion involved more than simply winning games—it also involved understanding when to make the difficult decisions for the right reasons.

The baseball world reacted with a mix of reverence and regret. Although his amazing deliveries on the mound would be missed, fans appreciated his bravery in prioritizing his health and future.

Despite their sadness at his leaving, his teammates understood the toll the game had taken on him and supported his decision.

Sandy continued to be involved in baseball even after he retired, always eager to impart his expertise and passion for the game.

He took on the role of mentor to younger players, teaching them the value of striking a balance between self-care and passion in addition to pitching.

He demonstrated to them that being great was more than just breaking records—it also involved overcoming obstacles in life.

There was more to Sandy Koufax's tale than just victories, flawless games, and seasons filled with records.

It was also about overcoming adversity, being resilient, and making difficult decisions with dignity.

His choice to leave the spotlight at the pinnacle of his career and acknowledge that some battles were not intended to be won at the expense of one's health demonstrated a different sort of strength.

Sandy would go down in baseball history as one of the best pitchers of all time, but he would also be recognized as an exceptional athlete with remarkable moral qualities.

His struggles had made him a legend both on and off the field, serving as a constant reminder to everyone that true greatness frequently necessitates making tough choices for the right reasons.

Sandy Koufax had taken on his obstacles head-on and come out with a legacy that was not only unharmed but even more motivating.

The left-handed player had altered the game in numerous ways, and his legacy would motivate athletes for years to come.

CHAPTER 11: An Unforgettable Legacy

Even though Sandy Koufax retired from the mound at the pinnacle of his career, his influence on baseball remained.

His name would live on in stadiums, locker rooms, and the hearts of fans everywhere, even after he had retired.

The left-hander who possessed a lightning-fast fastball and an impeccable curveball had transformed people's perceptions of pitching, and his enduring influence only became more significant as time went on.

Even though his stats were good, Sandy's contribution to the game was much greater. With an incredible 2,396 strikeouts, four no-hitters, and a 2.76 career ERA, he concluded his career.

He was a three-time Cy Young Award winner, a seven-time All-Star, and the MVP of the World Series twice.

His list of accomplishments was infinite. An uncommon distinction for a pitcher, he even took home the 1963 National League MVP title.

Despite suffering from pain, he won another Cy Young Award during his penultimate season in 1966.

He had cemented his status as one of the best players of all time by the time he retired.

However, the statistics by themselves were unable to adequately convey Sandy's remarkable legacy.

Pitchers now approach the game differently because of him. Pupils observed his delivery, his windup, and his laser-like concentration on the mound.

They discovered that becoming a great pitcher required more than just throwing hard; it also required developing control, strategy, and mental toughness.

Every time a new lefty took the mound, observers couldn't help but ask themselves, "Is this guy the next Koufax?" Sandy also left behind a legacy of tenacity and fortitude.

It had not been an easy path for him. He had battled through agonizing ailments, self-doubt, and wayward pitches.

Nevertheless, he never gave up. Rather, he turned those setbacks into motivation to excel.

His narrative became an inspiration to those going through difficult times in their own life, not only baseball players. "Maybe I can too if Sandy Koufax can overcome it," they would reason.

Sandy was admitted to the Baseball Hall of Fame in 1972. He became the youngest player to ever achieve this award at the age of thirty-six.

He considered his career with humility as he stood at the Cooperstown podium, surrounded by the greatest luminaries in the history of the game.

He talked about the joy he found in the game and the honor of playing for the Dodgers, rather than his accomplishments or records.

He declared, "My passion was baseball, and I gave it everything I had." What I'm most proud of is that.

Sandy stayed a low-key figure in baseball even after being elected to the Hall of Fame. He didn't look for attention or strive for celebrity.

Rather, he devoted his time to coaching and imparting his knowledge to young pitchers. His guidance was regarded as invaluable by many players, and his composed, considerate manner made a lasting impact on everyone he encountered.

His typical response to questions concerning his pitching was to shrug and say, "I was just doing my job."

However, it was widely acknowledged that he had elevated pitching to a level of art. His integrity was among Sandy's most enduring qualities.

He had consistently upheld his moral principles, acting with integrity and regard for both the game and his principles.

That integrity was demonstrated by his decision to skip Game 1 of the 1965 World Series in observance of Yom Kippur.

Many were motivated by this move, which served as a reminder that sometimes sticking to your morals is more essential than winning.

Stories about Sandy's great plays, his flawless game, his unwavering perseverance, and his contribution to the team have been handed down through the generations of baseball fans.

Children played Sandy Koufax in backyards across America, imitating his windup and hoping to throw a pitch exactly like him.

Coaches utilized his career to model for new players the importance of perseverance, hard work, and humility.

The way Sandy left her mark on people's emotions, nevertheless, may have been its most lovely aspect.

To the innumerable spectators who saw him pitch, he provided joy, excitement, and optimism.

When he pitched that perfect game or knocked out eighteen batters in one game, people could still clearly recall where they were.

His matches were enchanted moments that brought spectators together in wonder and respect.

Sandy Koufax embodied everything that made baseball great and was always there when the game needed a hero.

Sandy's name remained revered even as the years stretched into decades. His accomplishments served as evidence of his greatness, and both players and fans continued to draw inspiration from his sportsmanship and moral qualities.

The saying "There will never be another Koufax" is used by baseball writers, analysts, and historians to recognize the special blend of talent, tenacity, and humility that made his career so remarkable.

But Sandy never cared about becoming a legend in his own right. It was about the pride in being a member of a team, the love of the game, and the thrill of pitching.

Not only did his records endure, but his influence endured in the minds and hearts of all pitchers who mounted the mound with hope and fire in their bellies.

Sandy Koufax had left a lasting impression on baseball, and the sport will always remember him.

He had demonstrated to the world that being great involved more than just winning; it also involved how one played the game, overcoming obstacles, and putting their all into each pitch.

In this way, the tale of Sandy Koufax would live on, encouraging upcoming generations to set lofty goals, put in a lot of effort, and play with unwavering enthusiasm.

CHAPTER 12: Lessons from Sandy

Throughout his baseball career, Sandy Koufax experienced many remarkable experiences, illustrious accomplishments, and motivating obstacles.

Apart from the fastballs, curveballs, and titles, Sandy also left behind priceless teachings that went well beyond the diamond.

His narrative served as a helpful reminder of what it takes to follow your passion, get past setbacks, and lead a moral life.

1. Hard Work Pays Off: Sandy put in a lot of effort to improve his baseball abilities from the time he first took up the bat as a young child in Brooklyn.

He struggled in numerous ways despite his innate talent, one of which was his early wildness on the mound.

But he refused to let those setbacks define who he was. Rather, he practiced diligently every day to develop control over his pitches.

Sandy showed us that hard work and perseverance are what make a champion—innate talent can only get you so far.

2. Never Give Up: There were highs and lows in Sandy's career. Many didn't think he would ever be a great player because of his wild and erratic early career pitching. Sandy persisted nonetheless.

He persevered through the difficult moments, growing from his mistakes and maintaining his resolve.

His tenacity serves as a potent message for everyone facing obstacles: great things are achievable if you believe in yourself and keep trying even though success doesn't come effortlessly.

3. The Power of Focus: Sandy was the epitome of focus on the mound. He learned to tune out outside noise and concentrate only on throwing the perfect pitch in front of thousands of screaming spectators in a crowded stadium.

He was able to get over his anxiety, pressure, and even pain with this focus. Sandy demonstrated to us the importance of maintaining focus on your objectives in the face of adversity.

4. Accept Your Challenges: One of Sandy's most motivational life lessons is how he overcame adversity to become stronger.

Because of his early control issues, he had to learn how to master his pitches, which made him a more astute and strategic pitcher.

He learned tenacity and the value of understanding one's limitations from his struggle with injuries.

Sandy accepted challenges rather than allowing them to hold him back, seeing each obstacle as a springboard to success.

He demonstrated to us that obstacles are chances for growth rather than barriers.

5. Integrity Is Important: Sandy has never wavered from his morals. He made choices that were consistent with his values and character, whether it was opting not to play on Yom Kippur or resigning at the pinnacle of his career to safeguard his health.

Fans, rivals, and teammates all respected and loved him for his integrity. Sandy's story serves as a reminder that success is determined more by our methods than by our accomplishments.

One of the most significant accomplishments of all is remaining true to who we are. 6. Be a Team Player: Sandy never placed himself above the group, even with his legendary position.

He understood that baseball was a team sport and that each member of the team, from the utility infielder to the star pitcher, contributed to the team's accomplishments.

He was always willing to encourage his teammates, giving younger pitchers guidance and acknowledging their accomplishments.

Sandy sets a good example for us all by emphasizing teamwork, humility, and putting the good of the group ahead of oneself.

7. Strike a Balance between Passion and Self-Care: Sandy made the tough but incredibly wise decision to retire at the age of thirty.

He understood that sometimes putting your health and well-being first is necessary, even if it means letting up on something you enjoy.

The decision he made is a powerful reminder that, in addition to pursuing your passion, it's critical to know when to listen to your body and take care of yourself.

8. Savor the Journey: Despite his laser-like concentration on the field, Sandy never forgot the happiness that baseball offered to him.

His passion for the game was evident in each pitch and each inning. He was playing because he enjoyed it, not only to get records or get famous.

Sandy serves as a reminder that real satisfaction comes from doing what you love, even in a society where winning is frequently prioritized over all else.

9. Inspire Others: Sandy was an inspiration to several baseball players and fans during his career.

He was an inspiration because of his poise under duress, his work ethic, and his sportsmanship.

He demonstrated that being great involves more than simply talent—it also involves one's demeanor and the effect one has on others.

His narrative inspires us all to be the kind of person who makes a positive impact on others and leaves a lasting legacy.

10. Never Stop Learning: Sandy never stopped seeking methods to get better, even at the height of his success.

He studied his opponents, refined his technique, and worked on new pitches. His commitment to education and development serves as a lesson to all of us: no matter how skilled you are in a given area, you can always learn more and improve.

There is more to Sandy Koufax's legacy than just statistics and records. It's a tale of fervor, tenacity, modesty, and the quest for greatness.

We are motivated to work hard, take on obstacles head-on, adhere to our principles, and always aim to be the best versions of ourselves by the lessons learned from his path.

Sandy taught us that living a great life and bringing your whole self to whatever you do matters just as much as your accomplishments.

Sandy's teachings will be a legacy for baseball players to come as they take the field.

They will never forget the legacy of the lefty who altered the course of history, whether they are cheering from the dugout, making a play, or tossing a pitch.

In that way, the memory of Sandy Koufax will live on, motivating athletes, dreamers, and anybody aiming for greatness by serving as a reminder that anyone can leave an enduring

legacy if they have the right kind of heart, drive,

and charm.

CHAPTER 13: Fun Facts About Sandy Koufax

Baseball star Sandy Koufax had a legendary career. However, his narrative is made even more extraordinary by a wealth of fascinating and entertaining facts about him that go beyond his on-field accomplishments.

These are some intriguing and unexpected facts about the left-handed player who altered the game!

1. Basketball Was His First Love: Sandy Koufax wasn't originally a baseball player, despite popular belief. His first love as a child, growing up in Brooklyn, was basketball!

In high school, he was a gifted basketball player, and many speculated that he may play professionally.

He even attended the University of Cincinnati to play basketball before opting to concentrate on baseball. What if he had selected hoops rather than the mound?

2. inked for a Sweet Deal: In 1954, Sandy received a $14,000 signing bonus when he inked his first professional deal with the Brooklyn Dodgers!

Back then, that was a big sum of money. He was referred to as a "bonus baby," a term used to describe rookies who had to be placed right onto the major league roster due to the size of their bonus.

That implied that he entered the major leagues without ever playing in the minor leagues!

3. Known as "The Left Arm of God":

Sportswriters and fans dubbed Sandy "The Left

Arm of God" because of how strong and accurate his left arm was.

It was a moniker that perfectly conveyed the admiration and respect that people felt for his pitching prowess.

He always had the impression that something extraordinary was going to occur when he got onto the mound.

4. A Record-Breaking Strikeout Machine:

Sandy's 382 strikeouts in a single season in 1965 set a Major League Baseball record that remained in place for a long time.

He struck out 14 batters in a perfect game he pitched against the Chicago Cubs on September 9, 1965. One of the best pitching efforts in baseball history is still regarded as having occurred in that contest.

5. A Man of Principle: Sandy made news in 1965 when he refused to pitch on Yom Kippur during the World Series, demonstrating his steadfast adherence to his religious beliefs.

It was a choice that won him admiration on and off the field from individuals of all backgrounds.

6. Sandy's Curveball: Sandy Koufax possessed a renowned curveball. Because of the way the ball would start high in the strike zone and then abruptly descend steeply as it approached the plate, batters would refer to it as a

"fall-off-the-table" pitch.

It became one of his most lethal weapons since

batters could hardly hit it. Some people

compared hitting Sandy's curveball to trying to

hit a balloon that bursts unexpectedly!

7. Left-Handed, Right-Handed: Sandy pitched

left-handed, but he also performed a lot of things

right-handed. With his right hand, he wrote, ate,

and even played basketball. But his left arm was absolute magic when it came to baseball!

8. An Early Retirement: Sandy's 30-year-old retirement startled the baseball community.

He was at the height of his career but decided to retire due to severe arthritis in his left elbow.

His choice to put his long-term health ahead of his on-field achievements and continued notoriety was regarded as very bold.

9. The Youngest Hall of Famer: Sandy Koufax became the youngest player to ever be elected into the Baseball Hall of Fame in 1972 when he was just thirty-six years old.

For a guy who had accomplished so much in a relatively short career, it was a well-deserved distinction.

10. A Man of Few Words: Sandy was regarded as a reserved and modest person. He didn't chase attention or like the spotlight that accompanied his stardom, in contrast to many other sports stars.

He kept his personal life secret and let his pitching do the talking. He frequently played down his accomplishments in interviews, claiming he was just carrying out his duties.

11. A Mentor to Many: Sandy continued to be active in baseball after retiring, particularly serving as a mentor to up-and-coming pitchers.

He would share his experiences, give guidance, and aid in the skill-building of others. Sandy was credited by many players who followed him with assisting them in comprehending the mental and physical components of pitching.

12. No-Hitter King: Sandy Koufax

accomplished the amazing achievement of

pitching four no-hitters during his career.

The perfect game he pitched in 1965, in which

no opponent reached first base, was his fourth

no-hitter.

Even now, one of the greatest feats in baseball

history is still pitching four no-hitters.

13. Sandy the Scholar: Sandy first enrolled at the University of Cincinnati to pursue a degree in architecture. He didn't decide to devote himself to baseball full-time until after graduation.

Who knows, maybe instead of hitting batters out of the park, he would have been designing structures!

14. Always Modest: Sandy never wavered in his humility about his talents, even in the face of his extraordinary success.

"I was fortunate to be in the right place at the right time and to have teammates who supported me,"

he once remarked. Fans loved him even more because of his modesty. He was one of the all-time great pitchers, yet he never behaved like a superstar.

15. Inspiration for Future Generations:

Players and spectators have been motivated by Sandy Koufax for many years.

He demonstrated that you can succeed in any endeavor and overcome any challenge if you are committed, diligent, and have a passion for the game.

Youngsters who aspire to play baseball frequently look up to Sandy because of his graceful, modest, and heartfelt style of play as well as his incredible stats.

These interesting facts demonstrate that Sandy Koufax was a remarkable individual who led an event-filled life in addition to being a fantastic player.

Despite having a shorter career than most, he had many inspiring, challenging, and brilliant moments. In the baseball world, Sandy Koufax is and always will be a legend.

GLOSSARY

Baseball has its distinct lingo, full of expressions that add excitement and enjoyment to the game.

This dictionary of words can help you better comprehend baseball, particularly about Sandy Koufax's amazing career!

1. Ace: A baseball team's finest beginning pitcher. The Dodgers' ace, Sandy Koufax, guided the group with his exceptional plays.

2. All-Star: A player selected to participate in the annual All-Star Game who is deemed to be among the best in the league. Throughout his career, Sandy Koufax was named an All-Star seven times.

3. Arthritis: An ailment that results in joint discomfort and inflammation. Sandy Koufax had arthritis in his left elbow, which ultimately caused him to retire early.

4. Batter: The player that attempts to hit the ball that the pitcher throws while standing at home plate. Because of Sandy Koufax's brilliance and speed, batters frequently dreaded confronting him.

5. Bonus Baby: A term used to describe rookies who had to be added straight to the major league roster in exchange for large signing incentives. When Sandy Koufax joined the Dodgers, he was considered a "bonus baby".

6. Breaking Ball: A pitch that alters course or curves as it gets closer to the hitter. Throughout baseball history, one of the most well-known breaking pitches is Sandy Koufax's curveball.

7. Curveball: A pitch that, as it approaches the hitter, turns and curves downward. Sandy gained a reputation as one of the best pitchers in the game thanks to his razor-sharp curveball, which left hitters swinging at the air.

8. Cy Young Award: Each year, the American League and National League's top pitchers are recognized with this award. Throughout his career, Sandy Koufax was a three-time Cy Young Award winner.

9. Dugout: When the players and coaches are not on the field, they sit on this side of the field. Between innings, Sandy would sit in the dugout and get ready for his next turn on the mound.

10. Earned Run Average (ERA): This is a statistic that evaluates a pitcher's performance based on how many runs they give up on average every nine innings. With a remarkable lifetime ERA of 2.76, Sandy Koufax demonstrated his supremacy on the mound.

11. Fastball: A fast pitch is thrown quickly, frequently exceeding 90 mph. Fastballer Sandy Koufax was known for his lightning-fast and pinpoint accuracy, which made it hard for hitters to hit.

12. Hall of Fame: The best players, managers, and innovators in baseball are recognized and honored in the Cooperstown, New York,

Baseball Hall of Fame. In 1972, Sandy Koufax became one of the youngest players in history to be inducted into the Hall of Fame.

13. Inning: A phase of the game in which every team takes turns fielding and hitting. In baseball, a typical game lasts nine innings. Sandy frequently completed nine innings of work when pitching a full game.

14. Lefty: A left-handed player's nickname. Pitcher Sandy Koufax was a southpaw with a strong left arm.

15. Major Leagues : Major League Baseball (MLB) in the US and Canada is the top division of professional baseball. Playing for the Brooklyn and Los Angeles Dodgers in the major leagues was Sandy Koufax.

16. Mound: The elevated space where the pitcher stands to toss the ball in the middle of the baseball field. Pitcher Sandy Koufax dominated games from the mound, hitting batters with his strong deliveries.

17. No-Hitter: A pitching match in which the opposition is unable to muster a single hit. Throughout his career, Sandy Koufax pitched four no-hitters, including a perfect game.

18. Perfect Game: An uncommon feat in which a pitcher pitches nine innings to 27 batters and no one reaches base. On September 9, 1965,

Sandy Koufax pitched a perfect game against the Chicago Cubs.

19. Pitcher: The athlete who tosses the ball from the mound to the batter. Known for his fastball and curveball, one of the all-time great pitchers was Sandy Koufax.

20. Relief Pitcher: A pitcher who enters the game after the winning pitcher, either to give the starter a break or in situations where the starter is having trouble. Sandy Koufax started the game on the mound almost all the time as a pitcher.

21. Rookie: A player participating in their major league debut. In 1955, Sandy Koufax was still a rookie for the Brooklyn Dodgers.

22. Shutout: A pitching performance in which the opposition side is unable to score any runs. Throughout his career, Sandy pitched multiple shutouts, including some of the biggest games, such as the World Series.

23. Strikeout: An out is declared when a batter fails to hit the ball after three strikes. Sandy Koufax was renowned for his ability to strike out batters; he finished his career with 2,396 strikeouts, numerous times leading the league.

24. Strike Zone: The area where the pitcher wants to deliver the ball over home plate, between the batter's knees and the middle of their torso. Pitching in the strike zone with a combination of quickness and accuracy to get hitters out, Sandy was an expert.

25. World Series: The American League and National League winners of Major League Baseball square off in this championship series. In addition to leading the Dodgers to many Series wins, Sandy Koufax was twice awarded the MVP of the World Series.

This glossary offers an insight into the amazing career of Sandy Koufax and the interesting world of baseball.

You may appreciate the talent, strategy, and thrill of the game that turned Sandy into a legend more fully if you keep these terms in mind. You'll comprehend what makes baseball, and players like Sandy Koufax, so unique, whether you're taking the mound, hitting the ball, or just watching from the stands.

This or That Baseball Fun!

Before we wrap up the story of Sandy Koufax, let's have a little fun!

Here are some "This or That" questions to help you think about your favorite baseball moments and what you've learned about Sandy Koufax.

Circle or write down your choice for each question!

1.Fastball or Curveball?

2. Pitcher or Catcher?

3. Sandy Koufax or Jackie Robinson?

4. Night game or Day game?

5. Strikeout or Home Run?

6. Baseball cards or Baseball cap?

7. Dodgers' blue or Yankees' pinstripes?

8. Throwing a No-Hitter or Hitting a Grand Slam?

9. Grass field or Turf field?

10. First pitch or Last out?

11. Watching baseball or Playing baseball?

12. Dodger Stadium or Yankee Stadium?

13. Extra innings or Regular innings?

14. Baseball glove or Baseball bat?

15. Winning the World Series or Winning a Cy Young Award?

16. Curveball that surprises the batter or Fastball that blows past the batter?

17. Sandy Koufax in his prime or A modern-day pitcher?

18. Hot dogs at the stadium or Popcorn at the stadium?

19. Pitching from the windup or Pitching from the stretch?

20. Practicing in the backyard or Playing in a big game?

Reflect and Share: Now that you've made your choices, think about why you picked each one! Feel free to write a few sentences about your favorite question.

Maybe you chose "Fastball" because you love the speed, or "Curveball" because it's tricky!

Bonus Challenge:

- Ask a friend or family member these questions to see how their answers compare to yours!

These "This or That" questions are a great way to celebrate the amazing moments in baseball and connect with Sandy Koufax's story before we conclude. Thanks for joining in on the fun!

CONCLUSION

The tale of Sandy Koufax is one of greatness, tenacity, and passion. His journey from impoverished Brooklyn origins to becoming one of baseball's most illustrious pitchers is proof of what it means to genuinely love the game.

Sandy persevered in the face of enormous obstacles, including wild pitches, injuries, and the spotlight pressure.

Rather, he accepted every challenge, put in more effort than before, and permanently altered baseball.

Sandy Koufax was a role model in addition to being an exceptional pitcher. For many players and spectators, he became a legend because of his commitment to hard work, his sportsmanship, and his honesty both on and off the field.

Sandy played the game with love and grace, whether he was throwing his trademark curveball or his scorching fastball.

He demonstrated to us all that hard work, perseverance, facing obstacles head-on, and putting the good of the group ahead of one's ego are all necessary for success.

Sandy's legacy inspired many long after he retired. Young pitchers throughout the world aspire to be as good as him and look up to him.

His amazing records, flawless games, and legendary performances are still spoken about by fans.

His tale is used by coaches to instill in their players the virtues of tenacity, humility, and playing for the love of the game.

Sandy Koufax's impact extends beyond his record and awards. His narrative serves as a helpful reminder that greatness may be found in both the results and the process of achievement.

It can be found in the bravery to stick to your morals, the humility to work well with others, and the perseverance to move on in the face of adversity.

Baseball history will never be the same because of the lefty who altered the game. Sandy demonstrated to us that, with enough effort and dedication, any goal can become a reality.

In doing so, he not only left behind records but also a legacy that will motivate sportsmen, aspirants, and everybody who enjoys the rush of striving for greatness in the future.

Thus, keep Sandy Koufax in mind the next time you witness a pitcher winding up on the mound.

Consider the young Brooklynite who gave his all to every pitch, persevered through every setback, and transformed baseball with his skill and morals.

Sandy's tale serves as a reminder that striving for greatness and having a passion for the game can result in extraordinary things. We should remember that lesson in life as well as on the pitch.

Made in the USA
Las Vegas, NV
02 March 2025

18951563R00120